Duke Ellington

Ambassador of Music

Duke Ellington, Ambassador of Music

by Pamela Barclay,
illustrated by Harold Henriksen

Creative Education
Mankato, Minnesota 56001

Published by Creative Education, 123 South Broad Street,
P. O. Box 227, Mankato, Minnesota 56001
Text copyright © 1974 by Ann Mayer. Illustrations copyright © 1974 by Creative
Education. No part of this book may be reproduced in any form without written
permission from the publisher. International copyrights reserved in all
countries. Printed in the United States.
Distributed by Childrens Press, 1224 West Van Buren Street, Chicago, Illinois 60607
Library of Congress Number: 74-8211ISBN: 0-87191-367-4

Library of Congress Cataloging in Publication Data
Barclay, Pamela.
Duke Ellington; ambassador of music.
(Personal close-ups)
SUMMARY: A biography of the black musician who in
fifty years has composed 2000 songs and performed them
all over the world.
1. Ellington, Duke, 1899- —Juvenile literature.
(1. Ellington, Duke, 1899- 2. Musicians.
3. Negroes—Biography) I. Henriksen, Harold, illus.
II. Title ML3930.E44B3 785.4'2'0924 (B) (92)
ISBN 0-87191-367-4   74-8211

INTRODUCTION

Duke Ellington's life is the story of a man who was determined to be someone someday. By high school, Duke had learned to play the piano and had formed his own band. When the band wasn't playing, its members would practice or listen to other bands. They were determined to be the best.

In 1920 Duke Ellington and his band left Washington, D. C. for New York. There Duke continued his pattern of hard work. Soon his band was recognized as one of the best. Through records and radio, the Ellington sound became nationally known.

Duke Ellington died on May 24, 1974, at age 75. Thousands of friends and music lovers bid a final farewell to the Duke at the Cathedral of St. John the Divine in New York. Duke's love of music and performing kept him working until a few weeks before his death. His personal presence shaped jazz for over half a century. And his many compositions and unmistakable styling are contributions which will continue to speak to the music world for many centuries to come.

Duke Ellington Ambassador of Music

Hand-clapping, foot-tapping, spirit-lifting music was his specialty. For over 50 years, Duke Ellington had his own band. He wrote over 2,000 songs. He took ragtime, jazz, blues, and black spirituals, fused them together and created the Ellington sound.

"As I travel from place to place by car, bus, train, plane....taking rhythm to the dancers, harmony to the romantic, melody to the nostalgic, gratitude to the listener....receiving praise, applause and handshakes, and at the same time, doing what I like to do, I feel that I am most fortunate...."

Edward Kennedy Ellington was born in Washington,

D.C., on April 20, 1899. His father, James, worked as a butler—a job familiar to many blacks at that time. While Mr. Ellington was a butler at the White House, he never dreamed that one day his son would be the honored guest of 4 presidents.

Daisy Ellington, Edward's mother, was a strong woman who made a fine home for her husband and their only son. In spite of white prejudice, Daisy taught her son to love life and live with class. The house in northwest Washington was often a gathering place for family — aunts, uncles and dozens of cousins. Good times and stories of the past made Edward proud to be an Ellington.

Edward went to church twice every Sunday. His mother would take him to services at her Baptist church, and his father would insist that Edward go with him to the Methodist church. Edward learned the songs and messages well, even though it was a lot of church for a very active young boy.

Edward loved to listen to his mother play the piano and wanted to learn how to make music himself. When he was 7, the Ellingtons agreed to let Edward take lessons from Mrs. Klingscale. The sounds he made weren't like his mother's music. He had to learn scales, chords and finger exercises. It took work, and it took time. Edward loved playing with the kids on R Street. There was always something to do, particularly at piano-practice time.

Edward was quickly becoming known as Duke. By the time he was 8, his friends were beginning to forget that his real name was Edward. He looked like a Duke. His shirt always matched his jacket. His pants were pressed and creased. His shoes were spit-shined till they looked like mirrors. In the morning, he would announce himself to his family by proclaiming, "Now look at me. Someday I'm going to be someone." Then he'd race off to school.

It was fun being part of the R Street gang. But it was hard work to practice and get the music to sound good. Duke usually chose the fun over the practice, but Duke's mother remained firm. When it was time for practice, she would often have to break up a baseball game to get him to come home and sit down at the piano.

By the time Duke started high school, there were new excitements in silent movies and fast cars. Duke and his R Street friends dreamed about the excitement of racing cars and spent many hours watching the adventures of silent movie heroes. Duke and his friends soon began to dress like their favorite stars. But occasional scuffles with white boys never let them forget that they lived in the black section of Washington.

At Armstrong High School, Duke became interested in art. He was good, and he was soon being asked to make posters for school programs. He entered an NAACP (National Association for the Advancement of Colored People) poster contest and won. During his last year at Armstrong Duke was offered a scholarship to Pratt Institute of Art in Brooklyn, New York; but he turned it down.

Music was no longer just hard work. Duke had mastered the basics, and he wanted to become a "somebody" in music. After he met Henry Grant, a music teacher at Dunbar High School who helped him with harmony, Ellington learned fast and was soon able to chord his own melodies.

The ragtime sound had caught hold of the country, and Duke was determined to master the new sound. He would practice two or three hours a night. Mr. Pinn, a neighbor of the Ellingtons, complained that his practicing was pretty tiresome to listen to. Duke kept right on practicing. "One of these days I'm gonna be famous," he would tell Mr. Pinn.

One day he told Pinn that he was going to start a band. Pinn knew some people who wanted a small band for a house party. Duke brought his R Street friends, Arthur Whetsol, Otto and John Hardwick and Jerry Rhea, together to form the first Ellington band. With Mr. Pinn's help they got their first job.

After the party Pinn told Duke, "Those folks were carried away with your music." That was all the band needed. They were always together. They would meet and talk music at the corner drugstore. They would practice until they had the right sound. And they would sit on a porch talking, planning and dreaming about their band.

Whenever possible Duke would listen and watch the ragtime professionals. He would come home and practice until he could do it just as they did. Duke practiced and practiced until he had a flashy left hand like the best ragtime piano players he had heard.

There were good times at house parties. There was plenty of ice cream and, of course, music. Duke had such a liking for ice cream that one of his first pieces was called "Soda Fountain Rag." Some of these house parties charged admission to help pay the host's rent. Duke was always in the middle of the guests, testing his skill on his raggy piano.

Sometimes Duke played with other Washington bands. There were jobs every weekend, so Duke and his friends soon began making money regularly. He was playing so often and making so much money, that he decided to leave high school a few months before graduation. This gave him more time to work at his music.

Duke put an ad in the yellow pages of the Washington Directory to get jobs at better places. Soon the Ellington band was making it as big as any band in the area. Even though there was always work for the band, Ellington would

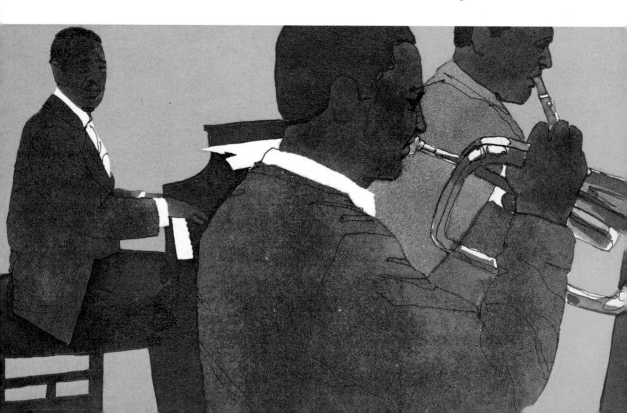

often paint signs for extra money.

After every job, Duke and his friends would talk about the sound of their music. The band loved to play and experiment even when they were the only ones to hear their sounds. They were developing confidence in their own abilities.

In Washington, it seemed only natural to plan big. The Ellington band always tried to do something bigger and better today than they had done yesterday. Excellence was becoming a way of life for Duke.

Mr. Duke Ellington and Miss Edna Thompson began seeing each other often. Edna was a young woman from the R Street neighborhood. In 1918 Edna and Duke were married. A year later Duke's son Mercer was born.

At the same time Duke met Sonny Greer, a drummer. Sonny soon joined the band. Greer knew the music world of New York. The Band wanted to make it in New York;

and, with the help of Greer, they got a job there. But when the first job ended, there were no more offers.

Duke, Otto, Arthur, Elmer and Sonny split a hot dog five ways and returned to Washington. They worked steadily and saved their money for another try in New York.

They went back in 1920, determined to stay. In New York, there were many new musicians using instruments in different ways, and there were always exciting sounds in the streets to catch their ears. Duke took it all in. He listened and sorted out what he heard. He was discovering the musical sound he had been looking for.

Duke and his band had several jobs in black Harlem. The people who heard him liked his sound, but big time meant making it in the white clubs of New York. Duke got a big break when the band was hired to play in the white Kentucky Club.

He was well liked. His music was good, and the elegant Duke charmed everyone he met. Other musicians began to drop in to hear the Ellington band. It was a good feeling to see other musicians do what he had done for so many years.

The excitement of the 1920's matched the sounds of jazz. White people were curious about the "new Negro" music. The night club audiences wanted to hear African melodies. They found the drums exciting and colorful. Duke was careful about his music. While he wanted his audience to like his music, he would not change the Ellington sound simply to be popular. Sounds had to make sense to him and add meaning to his music.

Many of the songs he wrote came from church songs. Other melodies came from the black folk tradition, and some melodies came just from reading street signs out loud. Duke and his friends would walk along and read out loud. They would stretch the sounds of the words into song-like shapes.

The band was growing. By 1923 they added more trumpet players, a trombone player and a wind bass player. That year they had their first recording date. The first records were made for a company which sold mostly to the South and to the black ghettos of the North.

In 1926 Duke met Irving Mills, a businessman. With Mills, the band grew into a big business. Duke became the president of the band, and Irving Mills was treasurer.

Mills set up recording dates with big record companies such as Columbia. He arranged for all the other things Duke's band did for the next 13 years. He even brought it to radio in 1926.

In 1927, Victor, the biggest record company, made the band an offer. Duke and Mills accepted.

The band recorded many of the early songs Duke had written. Among them were "Creole Love Call," "Black and Tan Fantasy," "The Blues I Love to Sing," and "Washington Warble."

Records gave many people a chance to hear Duke's music. He could present his band at its best in recordings.

Duke took advantage of this opportunity. He put the sounds of his world on records. He built up an audience as fast as he could record.

Duke's music always catches the listener. There are rich harmonies, fresh ways of using instruments, the growls of trumpets and trombones. There is the soft wailing of a saxophone; and there is a strong, heavy beat.

The early years of establishing the Ellington band were filled with pressures. These were difficult times for Duke and his wife Edna. It became increasingly difficult for them to understand one another. They grew further apart and isolated from each other's dreams. In 1926 they ended their marriage.

After the collapse of Duke's marriage, his parents moved

to New York with his sister Ruth, who was born when Duke was sixteen. They also brought Duke's son Mercer with them. Mercer had been living with the older Ellingtons in Washington. Now Duke and his family were together again. He felt happy and secure with them.

The band was his second family. Duke always shared his good fortune with those around him. He enjoyed giving. At Christmas Duke became Santa to the whole band. They would be invited to Duke's apartment where presents and good times were shared.

In 1927 the Ellington Band opened at the Cotton Club. At that time the Cotton Club was the best. It was a center for whites looking for the best in black music and in outlawed liquor. Run by bootleggers, the Cotton Club frequently changed its show to keep the regulars coming back. It was a white club where only the most famous blacks were permitted to spend their money out front with the whites. Most blacks who wanted to hear Duke had to stand back-stage.

The Cotton Club was a new challenge for Duke. The band had grown to twelve. They needed a steady stream of fresh music to keep the customers coming back. The ever-changing singers, dancers and chorus lines always needed new music. Radio broadcasts of the Cotton Club shows created new demands for Ellington records.

Ellington soon became a master at recording on 78 rpm records. The 78's permitted very little flexibility. There was room for only three minutes of music. Ellington had to write music which could work its magic in a very short time, and he learned to do it well.

Duke stayed at the Cotton Club until 1931. At that time interest in jazz seemed to be fading. People were beginning to listen to new sounds. Duke's future didn't appear very bright.

In 1933 the Ellington Band was booked for a European tour. The band looked forward to the work and to their first trip overseas. They believed that color didn't separate people in Europe as it did in America.

While the British called Duke the master of jazz, they would not give the band hotel rooms. Duke's band was finally able to stay at private boarding houses. Ellington and his band were insulted, but their music was eagerly accepted. Duke met and made friends with the Prince of Wales and Prince George.

The band traveled to Paris. The French loved Ellington's music. Although Duke was angered by the same senseless prejudice that he was forced to live with in America, the success of his music helped him go on.

After the European tour, Duke's manager Mills arranged for a tour of the South. Duke had said at one time that he would not go South because black people were treated so badly there. But after the success in Europe, he was willing to try. It proved to be worth the try. The band was welcomed everywhere. In Texas, the band was hailed as the greatest of the day.

The happy feelings soon evaporated. In 1935, Duke's mother was very ill with cancer. She refused to worry about herself. She was only worried about how Duke was doing. Duke spent the last three days of her life next to her bed, never leaving her. Her death was a terrible shock to Duke. He told his friends he had no interest in anything. He could see no future.

He turned to his music for comfort and hope. He wrote "Reminiscing in Tempo," a long piece to express his thoughts. Its sad, mournful thoughts slowly give way to hopeful ones. Although his mood did not become joyful, at least he had found hope in his work.

A new fad called swing was catching hold. It was a sound

which came from whites. It seemed a little like a used tennis ball; it bounced around a lot, but it did not have a powerful sound. Big bands began selling it, and soon everyone began saying that it was how a tune should go.

Along with the new sound came "jive talk." This was a new way of naming things. It was like the code language which earlier jazz groups used. Musicians used it, and then it caught on with other people. A bass became a "dog house," a clarinet was a "licorice stick," and a trombone was called a "slush pump."

Duke was left out of swing. This was one sound that his band did not help to create. When Duke's band played at the Chicago Congress Hotel, the critics came to listen. They heard the creative ways that Duke used his band. They knew that he was special among all the popular band leaders. Once more, Duke was on top.

His music always speaks for the black traditions. He never left the blues melodies, the gospel tunes, and what he calls the "black folk element" out of his music.

The last years of the 1930's brought more changes. Duke lost his father in 1937; and in 1940, Arthur Whetsol died. Arthur, Duke's boyhood friend, had been with the band from the beginning. Duke broke up his association with Mills in 1939. Mills had not been spending enough time with the band in the last few years.

Duke was eager to expand his music. He wanted to write a major piece that would tell the history of the American

Negro in music. He started to work on his long, musical piece called "Black, Brown and Beige."

It was difficult to be a composer, band leader and piano player all at the same time, but Duke took on everything. Still, he was worried about being able to write down all the musical ideas he wanted to. Then he met Billy Strayhorn. Billy, nicknamed "Sweet Pea" by the band, was the ideal co-worker for Duke. Together, they turned out a large group of songs.

It was a musical friendship that lasted until Billy died in 1967. Billy wrote the words for many of Duke's songs. He wrote music and arranged many pieces for the band. Billy and Duke's song, "Take the A Train," became the band's theme song. The two men also did the famous "Mood Indigo."

After the years of living with the swing fad, Duke went on to other musical goals. He gave his first concert in Carnegie Hall. It was a great success. In the next year, there were concert dates in Boston, Philadelphia, Cleveland and Los Angeles. Since the late 1940's Duke kept up an amazing schedule of tours and concerts. In 1950 there was another European tour. In 1965 Duke and his band were a triumph at the Newport Jazz Festival. Duke's boyhood dreams of fame had really come true. He appeared on the cover of *Time* magazine. In another European tour in 1958 Duke was presented to Queen Elizabeth II.

He wrote his first film score in 1959 for the film *Anatomy of a Murder.* In 1960 he wrote music for another film called *Paris Blues.* He gave a piano concert at The Museum of Modern Art in New York in 1962.

Another goal was reached in 1963. Duke wrote a show called "My People." It was written for the Century of Negro Progress exposition in Chicago. In this show, he expressed in music and dance the history of the American Negro for the last 100 years.

Duke was chosen by President Kennedy to represent our country on a tour of eastern countries in 1963. Duke and his band were ambassadors to Syria, Jordan, Afghanistan, India, Ceylon and Pakistan. At press meetings on these tours Duke was always asked questions about race. Duke would say that there was too much to answer, and to give only half an answer would be unfair to everyone, both black and white.

In 1965 Duke Ellington was invited to compose a sacred concert to be given at Grace Cathedral in San Francisco. He wanted this to be the best concert he had ever done. "I am not concerned with what it costs. I want the best of everything possible. I want the best singers and coaches . . . and I want them to give the best they have."

Duke wanted to write music of great reverence and beauty for this concert. He told himself, "You can't slouch, man. You've got to write stand-up-straight music for a cathedral." Duke translated his belief to music and stood up straight. Everyone was stirred by the beauty of his music.

After the performance at Grace Cathedral, Duke went on tour and brought his music into the holy places of all major religions around the world.

In 1966 Duke was asked to represent the United States at the World Festival of Negro Arts in Dakar, Senegal, Africa. In 1967 the African nation of Togo included Duke Ellington in a series of stamps commemorating the world's greatest composers. An audience of 7,500 people came to the Cathedral of St. John the Divine in New York City for the presentation of Ellington's second sacred concert. Three choirs helped the Ellington band perform the new music.

Duke had his 70th birthday party at the White House in 1969. When President Nixon made a toast to Duke and

asked him how he liked being at the White House, Duke simply said, "There is no place I would rather be tonight, except in my mother's arms."

On that night Duke was presented with the Medal of Freedom. It is the highest award our country gives in honor of outstanding men. When Duke Ellington accepted the award, he gave a list of four freedoms he lives by—first, freedom from hate; second, freedom from self-pity; third, freedom from fear of doing something that would help someone else more than it does himself; and fourth, freedom from the kind of pride that would make him feel he was better than his brother.

People were always amazed by Duke's busy schedule. He could have retired from such hard work long before he

died, but he had no plans to do so. He said, "I just dream and write. And I keep thinking that the thing coming up tomorrow is the big one. Who knows what direction it will take? What is there to retire to? My band and I travel all over the world, see the sights and see the people. You can't beat that. The road is my home, and I'm only comfortable when I'm on the move. New York is just where I keep my mailbox."

In Duke's offices in New York City the walls were lined with cups, plaques and awards. He was honored by four U.S. Presidents, by Queen Elizabeth II and by Pope Pius XII. He led the orchestras of London, Paris, Stockholm and Toronto. Many universities have given him degrees. Degrees are wonderful, he said, but the only reward he wanted to hear was his music.

In his hotel rooms there was always an electric piano for soft playing at night. Duke wanted to write down his ideas as soon as they came to him. His major concern was getting his music down. He wanted his music to last for a long time.

Right after the music was written he liked to record. Duke's method for many years had been to record new music, then take it home and listen to it. The next day he would make changes if he thought they were needed. Today the Ellington musicians rarely jam. Duke believed from many years of playing that the best of new and fresh sounds are written out in a score, or arranged.

Duke never liked to argue about what Jazz is. Because there are so many different styles, he felt that it was not right to put them all under one heading. Each musician makes his own style. Duke had always worked on his own Ellington sound.

When he led his band, Duke asked the players to give their heart and soul. When he wrote he tried to fit the music to the personality of the musician who will play. Many people asked Duke what good music is. Duke said "If it sounds good, it's good music; and if it doesn't, then it is not."

Duke was not worried about ratings or the "Top 40." He felt that if money is more important to an artist, then he is not true to his music. Without know-how, he said, nobody is anything. What is called good or best in the Top 40 should not be the only standard for a musician.

Duke always wrote songs that speak to people. He liked to remember things. Remembering, he said, helps him to write. He thought about things like old folks singing in the moonlight in the backyard on a hot night.

The Ellington band has stayed together longer than any other band. Duke was fair with his musicians. He would not discipline or argue with them. He said, "I don't believe in telling grown-ups to do things they should have learned when they were six years old."

Duke loved and respected his audience. He would never turn down someone who asked to hear one of his old songs,

no matter how many times he played it. If a song means something to people, then he felt he owed it to them to play it. "I respect the audience, and that means I can't be rude to them. I wasn't brought up that way, and I see no reason to change." Duke's respect for others brought him the respect and love of everyone who works with him.

In his long career Duke rose above prejudice. He was one of the first people to use themes of pride in black history. In 1938 he wrote a song called "Black Beauty." His answer to prejudice is in another song, called "What Color is Love, What Color is Virtue." He was proud of his show "My People," which tells of black history.

Duke always used the music of black people—ragtime, blues and gospel; but in all of the things he wrote, he added his personal elegance and grace.

Someone once asked Duke whether he got tired of writing and performing all of the time. His answer was a big NO. Music was always a source of happiness and growth for Duke. He always had new musical goals and worked hard to meet them.

Duke and music grew together. In 1973 Duke wrote a book about his life and the people he worked with. He called it Music is My Mistress. He had never wanted to take a vacation from what he liked doing more than anything else. This man who has written over 2,000 songs and performed all over the world could never imagine doing any-' thing other than composing and playing. Music was never tiresome for Duke Ellington because he loved it. It was his life.

Pamela Barclay

Having a bachelor's degree in applied music and a master's degree in music history, Pamela Barclay has pursued her interest in music since beginning piano lessons at age four. She teaches private piano, has worked as a musician and arranger in a small band, and contributed research materials for articles in music journals. Favorite avocations are writing poetry and short fiction, and training and riding horses.

Harold Henriksen

Harold was born in St. Paul, Minnesota and has lived there most of his life. He attended the School of the Associated Arts in St. Paul.

Even while serving in the Army, Harold continued to keep alive his desire to become an artist. In 1965 he was a winner in the All Army Art Contest.

After the Army, Harold returned to Minnesota where he worked for several art studios in the Minneapolis-St. Paul area. In 1967 he became an illustrator for one of the largest art studios in Minneapolis.

During 1971 Harold and his wife traveled to South America where he did on-the-spot drawings for a year. Harold, his wife and daughter Maria now live in Minneapolis where he works as a free lance illustrator.

Walt Disney
Bob Hope
Duke Ellington
Dwight Eisenhower
Coretta King
Pablo Picasso
Ralph Nader
Bill Cosby
Dag Hammarskjold
Sir Frederick Banting
Mark Twain
Beatrix Potter

close ups